SAVE THE CHILDREN

WITHDRAWN

RAINS

Virginia Loh-Hagan

45TH PARALLEL PRESS

Published in the United States of America by Cherry Lake Publishing
Ann Arbor, Michigan
www.cherrylakepublishing.com

Reading Adviser: Marla Conn, MS, Ed., Literacy specialist, Read-Ability Inc.
Cover Designer: Felicia Macheske

Photo Credits: © JC_Silver/Shutterstock.com, cover, 1; © Library of Congress, LC-DIG-anrc-16975, 5;
© Library of Congress, LC-DIG-stereo-1s20526, 6; © panitanphoto/Shutterstock.com, 11; © duncan1890/
iStock.com, 12; © Everett Collection/Shutterstock.com, 17; © Library of Congress, 12804v, 18;
© Susan Law Cain/Shutterstock.com, 21; © Library of Congress, LC-A6195- 6890, 22; © Vyntage Visuals/
Shutterstock.com, 25; © ilbusca/iStock.com, 29

Graphic Elements Throughout: © Chipmunk131/Shutterstock.com; © Nowik Sylwia/Shutterstock.com;
© Andrey_Popov/Shutterstock.com; © NadzeyaShanchuk/Shutterstock.com; © KathyGold/Shutterstock.com;
© Black creator/Shutterstock.com; © Edvard Molnar/Shutterstock.com; © Elenadesign/Shutterstock.com;
© estherpoon/Shutterstock.com

45th Parallel Press is an imprint of Cherry Lake Publishing.

Library of Congress Cataloging-in-Publication Data

Names: Loh-Hagan, Virginia, author.
Title: Save the Children : Orphan Trains / Virginia Loh-Hagan.
Description: Ann Arbor, Michigan : Cherry Lake Publishing, [2020]. | Series: Behind the Curtain | Includes index.
Identifiers: LCCN 2019032973 (print) | LCCN 2019032974 (ebook) | ISBN 9781534159433 (hardcover) |
    ISBN 9781534161733 (paperback) | ISBN 9781534160583 (pdf) | ISBN 9781534162884 (ebook)
Subjects: LCSH: Orphan trains–Juvenile literature.
Classification: LCC HV985 .L64 2020 (print) | LCC HV985 (ebook) | DDC 362.73–dc23
LC record available at https://lccn.loc.gov/2019032973
LC ebook record available at https://lccn.loc.gov/2019032974

Cherry Lake Publishing would like to acknowledge the work of the Partnership for 21st Century Learning,
a Network of Battelle for Kids. Please visit *http://www.battelleforkids.org/networks/p21* for more information.

Printed in the United States of America
Corporate Graphics

A Note on Dramatic Retellings

Participating in Readers Theater, or dramatic retellings, can greatly improve reading skills, especially fluency. The books in the **BEHIND THE CURTAIN** series give readers opportunities to learn about important historical events in a fun and engaging way. These books serve as a bridge to more complex texts. All the characters are real figures from history; however, their stories have been fictionalized. To learn more about the people and the events, check out the Viewpoints and Perspectives series and the Perspectives Library series, as the **BEHIND THE CURTAIN** books are aligned to these stories.

TABLE of CONTENTS

HiSTORICAL BACKGROUND

During the 1850s, thousands of orphans were living on the streets. They were living in big cities like New York City. They were poor. They didn't have food. They were homeless. They formed gangs. They robbed. They did whatever they could to survive. Some were taken to jails. Some were taken to orphanages.

The orphanages were overcrowded. They were unhappy places. Reverend Charles Loring Brace was in charge of the Children's Aid Society. He wanted to help. He wanted to give orphans a strong family life. He knew there were farmers in the rural Midwest. The farmers and pioneers needed help on their land.

Vocabulary

orphans (OR-fuhnz) children whose parents have died

gangs (GANGZ) groups that form to commit crime

orphanages (OR-fuh-nij-iz) shelters for orphans

rural (ROOR-uhl) having to do with country life or farming

Midwest (mid-WEST) the north-central part of the country

FLASH FACT!

The orphan trains traveled to over 45 states. Most went to the Midwest.

Vocabulary

placing agents (PLASE-ing AY-juhnts) people assigned to find homes for children on the orphan trains

adopted (uh-DAHPT-id) placed with a different family than your own to be raised by them

mistreated (mis-TREET-id) abused

foster (FAWS-tur) to care for another person's child for a while

So, Brace created a special program. His goal was to move orphans from big cities to homes in the Midwest. The orphans were moved by train. This became known as orphan trains. Placing agents rode with the orphans. They helped the children get adopted.

Between 1854 and 1929, the orphan trains moved over 200,000 children. The orphans were put on show. Families selected the orphans they wanted. Some children were placed in loving homes. Some were mistreated.

The orphan trains ended in the 1920s. States passed laws against placing children across state lines. They created government programs. They created a foster care system.

CAST of CHARACTERS

NARRATOR: person who helps tell the story

ANNA LANE: a **social worker** who becomes a placing agent

JAMES SINCLAIR: a 10-year-old orphan from New York City who is part of the orphan trains

GEORGE KING: a midwestern farmer who adopts James Sinclair

NANCY KING: the wife of George King

PREACHER: a religious person who preaches at a Methodist church

BACKSTORY
SPOTLIGHT BIOGRAPHY

Sister Mary Irene Fitzgibbon lived from 1823 to 1896. She was born in London, England. At age 9, she moved to Brooklyn, New York. She got sick. She almost died in 1849. In 1850, she became a nun. She taught in a church school. She saw the increase of orphans and homeless children. She saw babies die from lack of care. She saw babies left at church doors. She wanted to help. She collected money. She founded the New York Foundling Hospital in 1869. Foundlings are babies who have been abandoned. Fitzgibbon's hospital supported the orphan trains. She put a cradle by the door. She left the front door unlocked. Mothers could leave their children with no questions asked. They just had to ring the bell. The bell let the nuns know a baby was there.

Vocabulary
social worker (SUH-shuhl WUR-kur) a person whose job is to provide services such as food, housing, education, and health care to those who cannot help themselves

FLASH FACT!

Charles Loring Brace believed all children needed good homes, education, and jobs.

ACT 1

NARRATOR: ANNA LANE *is talking to* **JAMES SINCLAIR***.*
She's getting him ready for the orphan train.

ANNA: How long were you at the orphanage?

JAMES: Since Mama died. She had a terrible sickness. Papa tried to take care of me by himself. He works at the **docks** in New York City. But then, he got hurt. And he lost his job.

ANNA: That must have been tough.

JAMES: We ran out of money. We got kicked out of our room. Papa left me here at the orphanage. I wouldn't let his hand go. I begged him not to leave me. But he didn't listen.

ANNA: He didn't have a choice. He had to find work. He had to get well.

Vocabulary

docks (DAHKS) places by the sea where ships land and things are loaded and unloaded

FLASH FACT!

Many homeless children slept on the streets in New York City.

JAMES: He told me he'd come back. But he hasn't come yet. I'm trying to be brave. But I want to see my papa.

ANNA: I have sad news. Your papa passed away. He died from his **injuries**.

JAMES: So, I'm really an orphan?

ANNA: Yes. But I have good news for you. I'm going to take you on a special train trip. You're going to a better place. It's called Kansas.

JAMES: What's in Kansas?

ANNA: Your new family. How do you feel about that?

JAMES: I have a lot of feelings. I'm really sad about my papa. But I want to be in a family again. I don't want to live on the streets. Kansas just sounds so far away.

ANNA: It'll be better than this orphanage. You'll see.

Vocabulary
injuries (IN-joor-eez)
cuts and wounds

FLASH FACT!

Once chosen, boys and girls often helped out at their new parents' homes and farms.

NARRATOR: **GEORGE KING** *and* **NANCY KING** *live in Kansas. They're farmers. They're at their house.*

GEORGE: What did you do today?

NANCY: I went to the store. I saw an **advertisement**. Families are needed to care for orphans from New York. What do you think about that?

GEORGE: New York is far away.

NANCY: The orphans are being moved from New York to us. They're coming in trains.

GEORGE: I'm not sure. Why do you want a child?

NANCY: There are a lot of reasons. We don't have any children of our own. We're getting older. We could use help around the farm. And it would be nice to hear a child's laugh around here.

LOCATION SHOOTING
REAL-WORLD SETTING

The National Orphan Train Complex is in Concordia, Kansas. A complex is a bunch of buildings. The Complex is located at the old Union Pacific Railroad Station. It is a museum and research center. Its goal is to preserve the stories and artifacts of the orphan trains. It collects and shares information about the trains, orphans, and agents. It has exhibits. It has programs. It features orphans' stories. It has photos. It has educational materials. It has a restored train. Statues of orphans are all around Concordia. Over 4,000 people visit the Complex each year. Most of the visitors are orphan train orphans and their descendants. Descendants are people who are born from the same family line. The Complex wants people to remember what happened.

Vocabulary
advertisement (AD-vur-tize-muhnt) a notice or announcement in a public space promoting something

FLASH FACT!
Orphans ranged in age from 1 to 17 years old.

GEORGE: I'm just not sure.

NANCY: It'll be fine. Plus, our neighbors took in an orphan. And things are working out great for them.

NARRATOR: *It's Sunday morning.* **GEORGE KING** *and* **NANCY KING** *go to church. They're talking to a* **PREACHER***.*

PREACHER: We're **fortunate** to have orphan trains coming to our town.

GEORGE: Why is that?

Vocabulary
fortunate (FOR-chuh-nit) lucky

FLASH FACT!

Some orphans were excited to be chosen by families.

PREACHER: It's a chance for us to do God's work. We have a chance to help another soul.

NANCY: I told you, George. This will be good for us.

PREACHER: It's our duty to care for these young orphans.

GEORGE: Children are **expensive**. We'll have to provide food, clothing, and education.

NANCY: But we will get so much in return. The child can help us work the farm. And the child will brighten our lives.

PREACHER: If you're interested, we'll need to **interview** you. We have to make sure that you're a good fit.

GEORGE: What type of questions will you ask?

PREACHER: I'm sure you two will qualify. We just need to know about your job, property, and church attendance. We want to make sure you'll be good parents.

NANCY: We have so much to give. It would be great for us to share our home with a child who needs one.

GEORGE: Okay, let's do it!

Vocabulary
expensive (ik-SPEN-siv) costly

interview (IN-tur-vyoo) to ask questions to check for qualification

FLASH FACT!

Many interviews for potential families took place at churches.

ACT 2

NARRATOR: ANNA LANE *and* **JAMES SINCLAIR** *are on the orphan train.*

JAMES: Thanks for the new clothes, shoes, and haircut.

ANNA: Well, you have to look your best for your new family.

JAMES: Do you know who they'll be?

ANNA: Not yet. We'll find out soon. I'm sure you'll make a great **impression**. How are you enjoying the train ride so far?

JAMES: I've never left New York. I'm seeing things I've never seen before.

ANNA: Like what?

JAMES: Fields of corn. Apple trees. Yellow pumpkins. Lots of cows.

ANNA: What don't you like about the train ride?

JAMES: I'm getting tired of drinking milk and eating jelly sandwiches. It's also not very comfortable sleeping in my seat.

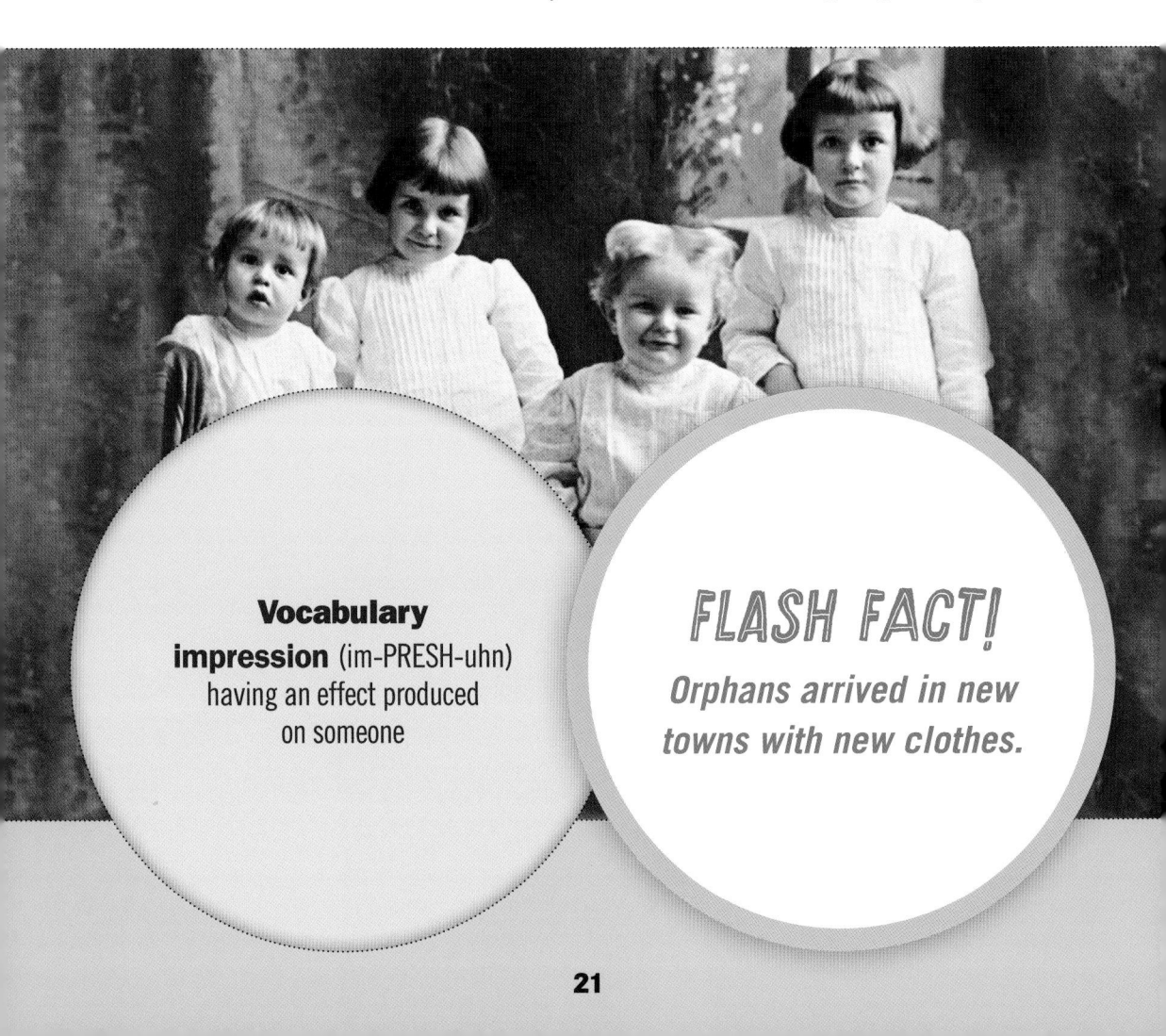

Vocabulary
impression (im-PRESH-uhn) having an effect produced on someone

FLASH FACT!

Orphans arrived in new towns with new clothes.

ANNA: We should be in Kansas soon.

NARRATOR: **ANNA LANE** *and* **JAMES SINCLAIR** *arrive in Kansas. They walk over to a nearby church.*

JAMES: There are so many people here.

ANNA: They're all here to meet you.

JAMES: Why are there chairs on that **stage**?

ANNA: You're going to sit on one of those chairs. Remember to sit up straight.

JAMES: Why do I need to do that?

ANNA: People are going to check you out. Come up when I call your name.

NARRATOR: *The* **PREACHER** *and* **ANNA LANE** *are on the stage. They're talking to the crowd that has gathered.* **GEORGE KING** *and* **NANCY KING** *are in the crowd.*

PREACHER: Our church welcomes Miss Anna Lane. We're looking forward to meeting the orphans.

Vocabulary
stage (STAYJ) a raised area

FLASH FACT!

Orphans lined up so potential parents could look at them.

ANNA: Thanks for supporting our **cause**. We're hoping to find good families for our poor orphans. These children have been through a lot. Some of them have had to search through trash for food. Some have slept in boxes. Now, they need good homes. They need to learn the Bible. They need to learn a **trade**.

PREACHER: The good people of this town have stepped up. We will help these children as best we can.

ANNA: First up is James Sinclair. He's 10 years old. He's healthy. He knows how to read and write.

Vocabulary
cause (KAWZ) an important belief, a reason worth fighting for
trade (TRADE) job skills

FLASH FACT!

Orphans learned new farming skills.

NANCY: Oh, George! Look at him. He seems perfect.

GEORGE: He's so scared. But he's trying not to show it.

NANCY: They're all scared and young. Poor things.

GEORGE: I heard that the Smiths took in an orphan. They treat the orphan like a **servant**.

NANCY: Some people are just bad. They're taking advantage of these orphans.

GEORGE: Hopefully, there are more good people than bad people. I want these orphans to go to good homes.

NARRATOR: *A group of men come onto the stage to examine* **JAMES SINCLAIR**. *One man squeezes his arm. Another man sticks his finger in his mouth to check his teeth.* **NANCY KING** *pulls James off the stage. She takes him away from the men.*

JAMES: You seem like a nice lady. Would you adopt me?

NANCY: I would love to. You can call me Mama King.

BLOOPERS
HISTORICAL MISTAKES

Many people didn't like the orphan trains. They thought they were abusing children. Some people took advantage of the system. Georgia Tann was one of them. She lived from 1891 to 1950. She studied piano. She studied law. But there weren't many jobs for women at that time. Tann ended up becoming a social worker. She was in charge of the Tennessee Children's Home Society. She sold white babies with blonde hair and blue eyes. She charged rich people a lot of money. She made up fees. She took the state's money. She didn't report her money to the U.S. government. But she did worse things. She stole over 5,000 babies. She tricked poor single mothers into giving up their babies. She took babies from women prisoners. She also kidnapped babies from day care. She took babies from hospitals and told unwed mothers that their babies had died.

Vocabulary
servant (SUR-vuhnt)
someone whose job is to serve

FLASH FACT!
Large groups of children traveled west on the trains.

NARRATOR: ANNA LANE *goes back to the train station. She and the* **PREACHER** *are **debriefing**.*

PREACHER: All the children got adopted today. I'm especially pleased about James and the King family. The Kings are a great couple.

ANNA: That is great news! I'll come back next year to check on the children. The children also know they can write to me.

PREACHER: I hope the orphan trains are successful. Children need to be protected and cared for.

Vocabulary
debriefing (dee-BREEF-ing)
talking about or recapping
the day's events

FLASH FACT!
Some orphans were
sent back to
New York because
the placement
didn't work.

EVENT TIMELINE

February 1853: Reverend Charles Loring Brace founded the Children's Aid Society. This group managed shelters for homeless people. It developed schools. It started the first free school lunch program in the United States.

October 1, 1854: The first orphan train arrives in Dowagiac, Michigan. It has 46 children ages 10 to 12.

May 20, 1862: President Abraham Lincoln signs the Homestead Act. The U.S. government gives free land to farmers. Farmers must live on the land for 5 years. They must improve the land. This inspires people to travel west.

1867: The first orphan trains arrive in Kansas. Between 5,000 and 6,000 children are placed in Kansas homes.

1868: Massachusetts begins "placing out" children. This system pays for families to take care of orphans instead of putting them in institutions. State officials must visit the foster homes.

October 8, 1869: The New York Foundling Hospital is set up. An orphan baby appears on the first night.

April 1901: Kansas passes laws about adoption. It orders the State Board of Charities to check out organizations placing children. William Stanley is the governor of Kansas. He says, "We cannot afford to have the state made a dumping ground for the dependent children of other states, especially New York."

1902: Anna Laura Hill applies for a job as a placing agent. She's the main agent for placing children in Kansas. She works at this job for 30 years.

April 9, 1912: The U.S. Children's Bureau is set up. Its goal is to protect children.

May 31, 1929: The last orphan train leaves New York City. It heads to Sulfur Springs, Texas.

1986: Mary Ellen Johnson works as a publisher's assistant. She starts the Orphan Train Heritage Society of America. This group hosts reunions for orphan train orphans.

CONSIDER THIS!

TAKE A POSITION! Were the orphan trains a good idea? Do you think they helped children or not? Argue your point with reasons and evidence.

SAY WHAT? Learn more about social workers. Interview a social worker. Find out what they do. Find out how they help their communities.

THINK ABOUT IT! Have you ever ridden a train? If so, describe what it was like. If not, would you consider it? Compare trains to cars and planes. What are the advantages of trains? What are the disadvantages of trains?

Learn More

Caravantes, Peggy. *The Orphan Trains.* Ann Arbor, MI: Cherry Lake Publishing, 2014.

Langston-George, Rebecca. *Orphan Trains: Taking the Rails to a New Life.* North Mankato, MN: Capstone Press, 2016.

Raum, Elizabeth. *Orphan Trains: An Interactive History Adventure.* Mankato, MN: Capstone Press, 2011.

INDEX

ABOUT THE AUTHOR

Dr. Virginia Loh-Hagan is an author, university professor, and former classroom teacher. Her favorite characters are orphans. She loves Anne Shirley, Cinderella, and Harry Potter. She lives in San Diego with her very tall husband and very naughty dogs. To learn more about her, visit www.virginialoh.com.